Empathy Rising

The Collected Poems of Steve McRoberts

Steve McRoberts

http://www.geocities.com/loyal2truth

Steve McRoberts
4/27/06

ISBN: 978-1-4116-8521-5

Published through Lulu, Inc.

3131 RDU Center, Suite 210

Morrisville, NC 27560

www.lulu.com

Printed in the U.S.A.

For Debi,

who found me when I was lost,
and brought love back into my world

Table of Contents

Introduction

It is with some trepidation that I send these poems out to face the world's acceptance and/or scorn. Good poetry can be sublime: bad poetry is embarrassing. For poets in love with their creations, sorting between the two can be a daunting task. In this collection, I hope that I have chosen well.

I believe that in these pages you will find something that will move you: whether it be to tears, joy, or thoughtfulness. Then, though it be time-shifted and location-shifted, we will have shared a bit of life between us: a bit of empathy: of hearts beating in harmony. It is for just such experiences that I read and write poetry. Indeed, it is for such experiences that I *live*.

Steve McRoberts

St. Paul, MN 2006

http://www.geocities.com/loyal2truth

Empathy Rising

The signs of life, both now and after:
a storm, the wind, the rain,
the taste of tears, the sound of laughter:
echoes of our lonely pain.

A cricket chirps beside my ear,
a flower opens in my heart,
replacing all the ancient fear
and granting us a brave new start.

The dawn is breaking, and the light
is driving out the old dark days.
The deaf can hear, the blind have sight;
we've found our way out of the maze.

In caring for the fragile Earth
we learn to share and give.
In seeking out each other's worth
we learn to love and live.

The priest is burying his gods.
The hunter's laying down his gun.
The angler's broken all his rods.
The deer are basking in the sun.

The soldier's coming home again;
while walking in another's shoes
he learned in war no one can win,
and used his moral right to choose.

When offering a helping hand
who knows what heights we'll reach?
With open arms and minds we stand
and love not *all* but *each*.

I feel you strong, I feel you weak:
I share your happiness and sorrow.
Your tear is coursing down my cheek,
my hope is tied to your tomorrow.

And when you take me by the hand
my heart is beating in the wild.
And when you say you understand
then once again I'm just a child.

In harmony, like stanzas rhymed,
or kindly deeds surprising,
we find our hearts and minds are primed
— our empathy is rising.

When First, My Love, We Meet

When first, my love, we meet,
we won't pretend or hide behind
clichés grown old and obsolete;
we'll see each other's heart and mind.

Our eyes and words may ricochet,
but I'll know you and you'll know me
not by looks or what we say
but through our hearts' own honesty.

It's not perfection that we'll seek
to make one gasp in idoled awe;
but just what makes us both unique:
our life, our truth, our every flaw.

Darkness and Light

Secure, I heard the days go by;
I could not *see* them *quite* —
a blind spot lay before each eye
and blocked out all the light.

Now, in such darkness oft there creeps
into the shadowed mind
the questions that the memory keeps
from times we've left behind.

It asks and tells what must be said:
the truth that all shall face,
what lies within must lie ahead:
"Is life a wall or space?"

But I have shunned the question long
and dared not touch or feel
for fear I'd touch a wall so strong
my blood would all congeal.

I let it trickle uselessly
for life seemed easier
without a light by which to see
I felt myself secure.

And then she came — a shining light
to show me life is real.
She came to me and gave me sight
of all I would conceal:

The emptiness before my face —
my ignorance destroyed.
But as her light had *shown* the space,
it also *filled* the void.

For Debi, My Bride

Dreams there were, of piercing strength,
which haunted lonely nights,
and stretched imagination's length
by wild and fancy flights.

All my life I've had such dreams
of very special places.
With golden mountains, silver streams,
and bright, enchanting faces.

Long I've sought this shining vision,
but always I've been turned away.
All my hopes met with derision,
my aspirations with dismay.

But then, into my life you came,
bringing sun, and light, and laughter!
Within my heart you lit a flame
which burns forever after.

You took my hand and led my high
and showed me all there was.
And when I asked you, "why?",
like a child, you said, "because".

You showed me all within your heart,
so passionate, and yet serene,
and there was love in every part,
and dazzling beauty in-between.

I know your faults, and all your charms,
that's why I love you in extremes.
And here within your gentle arms
I've found the place I sought in dreams.

Dave

My name - it don't matter - but just call me Dave.
I rose from the ashes of somebody's grave.

When I was a young man I most liked to dream
of castles made out of cake and ice-cream.

I'd plan and I'd figure and spend all my days
in tower, in dungeon, in labyrinth maze.

But as I grew older, my thoughts they did turn:
with women my passion did fire and burn.

I thought how to catch me a wondrous maid:
a pearl of fair beauty, with green eyes like jade.

The story is old, but as true as can be,
of how I did court her and how she loved me.

I slew all the dragons, I killed all her foes,
with dagger, with lance, with hand-to-hand blows.

Then locked in embrace, away how we flew
on magical carpet to our rendezvous:

a palace so grand, made of silver and gold,
where lightly the days, how they bounced, how they
rolled!

The Black Girl to the Jehovah's Witness

Written by Cynthia Rose for Ted Evanston (both character in my book, "Falling in Truth")

Will you love a laywoman's human bones?"
Or would you rather hold those old beliefs
that make all women Virgin Mary clones,
and study, lawyer-like, your own dry briefs,
while my hexagon of lips salivate?
Let's plead eternal guilt to nature's laws
and judge our case "desire insatiate".
Forget your proverbs, sayings, and old saws.
Just shape your tongue to fit me; I'm a bell -
and ring the watching stars from out their sockets:
rain gods, and devils! There's your heaven, hell,
and all the rest, aflame like streaking rockets!
That fire within you is not for God alone.
This black girl knows what black men want in prayer.
Their hunger wants no words, their bed no stone,
their thirst no salt, their ears no soundless air.
While belly, tongue, and ears have these needs,
there's something more than these he always craves,
as natural as the heart his lifetime bleeds:
he needs the tight confines of softest caves.
He needs the warming touch of tender lips.
And mine are yours for your still lips to hush
till all past joy and thought your flesh outstrips:
let's love so hard we'll make Jehovah blush!

Listen

Listen to the lies
gnawing gaping holes
like rats upon our souls.

Listen to the fights
as faith begins to shake
and hearts begin to break.

Listen to the hearts
as shadows fade
on the love not made.

Listen to the love
all but gone
with the light of dawn.

Then and Now

We lived on fiery passion then
which heated souls that walked in dreams
down shadow-mountains to a glen
where flowed, through blue, hypnotic streams,
an essence pure in liberty!
We drank the juice of freedom there
and found escape in poetry.
We lived a time beyond compare:
our souls were eyes which lit the night!
Our bodies melted into one
as we beheld the starry sight
in infinite oblivion!

And now, perchance, we meet sometimes.
In passing: nod, pretend to smile…
Forgotten are those walks and rhymes:
our words and selves go single-file.
And in the eyes we used in dreams,
and in our hearts which used to soar,
the fire of passion kicks and screams,
but heats and lights our souls no more.

Chance Reunion

How could you smile so hard
using speech four years old
(the length of our gut-stream
time has yanked from raw insides)?

How could I pretend so well
I was the same innocent boy
who blushed at every hint
and shrank from neutral touch?

How could we lie so frivolously:
"Nice to have seen you again,"
with you, your face pressed against heaven's vault,
and I, my arms enclasping earth?

How could the gods keep from laughing,
slapping each other on the back, pointing, joking,
as we paced apart our backs once more
pulling time in clenched teeth from one another:
"Look! Look! Two people who are lovers!"

Resurrection

Moldering peacefully underground
I have spent my days and hours
listening to the occasional sound
of women planting plastic flowers.

And often have I dreamed and thought
of the sky and clouds above my head
and how such beauty should be sought
before one lies here, cold and dead.

I wasted life in worried gloom:
daily my heart would shrivel and harden,
until the day you knelt on my tomb
and planted your flower garden!

I felt your patient fingers
working deep into the soil.
The smell of your sweat still lingers
as the sun shines on your selfless toil.

And once, I thrust a desperate arm
up through the dirt and rocks and roots:
To touch a petal, alive and warm –
I touched your love's own precious fruits!

And now to women who come to mourn
amongst the bodies scattered here,
I say, 'weep rather for those unborn
who'll hide their lives in constant fear.'

'For I have looked upon the light
of someone kind and true.'
Come brightest day or darkest night,
this is what I'll say of you.

A Memory

For Diane

Standing in our trailer-home
you felt so alone.
And still you would bake
love, disguised as cake.

Watching pink clouds at sunset
you were prettier yet.
I see you there still
standing at the windowsill.

Gazing in your liquid eyes
I know we lived in paradise.

Eulogy for us, because

For Mom

Eulogy for us, because
we've had none thus far
and those laurel and hardy times
laughing within too fine messes
shouldn't fade wordless.

Worrying through the night
about an incident real only to me
since only I recalled
a refused gift or possibility
and wondering what you did with that love
coming back from an off-handed neglect
of one who didn't realize
couldn't realize till some agonizing night
years later
that love was almost had.

Eulogy for us, because
if we lived at all
it was when we were together
and all the pulsing world
was a grave we played in
our play was love
and so the final act
eulogy for us, because
no matter what time says
we shall die together.

Father

We would've played football on Sundays
and I would've made the team.
We'd have gone to 'Father and Son Days'
and eaten hot-dogs, popcorn, and ice-cream…

And I'd have watched the mustard on your chin,
listening in awe as you belched up your beer,
and felt your razor-stubble as you'd grin
and hold me so near…

And I'd have made you very proud
dating cheerleaders and buying cars.
And I'd have been with the 'in crowd':
smoking, swearing, hanging around bars…

But when I was six months old

you left.

You gave me a body - but unsouled:

bereft.

And the void you left entered me:
a third-rate chess-player
stirring honey in his weak tea.
A dreamer, a would-be dragon-slayer…

I know when families are torn asunder
the deep wound heals quietly,
but do you ever wonder
just what became of me?
Or cry, or at least feel sad
that I never called you "Dad"?

The Idealist Who Wouldn't Let Go

I've seen the men without spirits walking.
They move slowly, without heat of passion.
And sometimes I've overheard them talking
of the weather or the latest fashion.

And to think you would have me be as they:
walking through my life some sort of zombie
with a vague awareness of night and day
sifting through like so much soot upon me.

And someone said, "A spirit is but light,
get your head out of the clouds: be a man!
Spirits will be broken be they ghost-white.
We'll get you work, and muscle, and tan.

And they put me to work at the millstone.
Every day we went around, around, around...
It, my unbroken spirit: I, its bone.
And as such, we to each other were bound.

It swung me about: I saw grassy sky!
I laid atop and it spun me dizzy.
I crawled inside and we hurled off to fly:
bounced over trees and skipped on the sea!

And someone said, "Stop day-dreaming and work!"
Said hateful things that made my heart hurt: Said:
"Get lost! Go to hell, you damn ugly jerk!"
Said: "I hate you and I wish you were dead!"

Now my millstone spirit has sunk so deep
it lies beneath this sea of sorrow.
Still bound, I pull and weep to see it sleep.
I thought we would fly forever, you know.

And you say, “Leave it there and swim ashore.
You re not pulling it up, but yourself down!”
But I’ve seen men without spirits before;
I’ll either come out with it, or I’ll drown.

Youth's Revenge

The layered landscape of my mind
has known no rest or peace
since scheming rebels and their kind
have plotted their release.

And in the darkest thoughts of all
amidst the sound of *Taps*
I've seen how they intend my fall
by glimpse at charts and maps.

They've massed together in my head,
a thousand strong and more.
I thought them spirits of the dead
come groping out death's door.
But no; they're people living still.
(In youth it all began,
when I would lean on windowsills
and see myself a man.
For there the seeds of men were sown,
from priest to judge to king
in time my future selves had grown.)
And now they're *thundering*!

To knights in armor I'm the foe;
the king's great enemy;
the trapeze artist's vertigo;
the priest's foul heresy.

I've slain no dragons — dreams I've flouted
I work, pay bills, drive cars…
and layers deep I hear it shouted:
"He's mad! Now victory's ours!"

The Masquerade

"Who am I?" Did you ask?
You want to see behind this strange mask?
Very well, I shall explain;
you see, I haven't always been the same.
Once I was so high above it all
I thought I could never fall.
For all the world was beneath me
and from it all I was set free.
But then came a time and took me by force
changing me into a star with no set course.
Soon my voice changed to soft, not loud,
while winds blew me about – a waterless cloud.
Now as you look at this face of mine,
let me show you a place and time
when everyone who looked at me
thought they saw an autumn tree.
But for a tree I am not suited,
having died twice and been uprooted.
I am a fountain with no water inside,
a fact I try to carefully hide,
for my mist has been driven away stormily
to become a foamy wild wave of the sea.
I'm like a rock and no higher.
A sow, just bathed, rolling in the mire.
And all that is reserved for me
is blackness and darkness eternally.

Now I see in your eyes that you resent
this description of my spiritual descent.
But soon we'll all take off our mask
and so, till then, please don't ask.

Baby Grand Piano

Written by Cynthia Rose, a character in my book, "Falling in Truth"

My sister died when I was nine.
Her piano standing mutely by
Like an open coffin, a fitting shrine
I'd lie within and daily die,
My little body thumping chords:
I laid in stiffness till they'd fade
And Satan came with all his hordes
To haul me off a simple shade.
But never did I pull it off;
Instead, my uncle plucked me hence.
He killed my mother with a cough
And brought me up in consequence.

Bob, you rescued me from that foul beast,
Enchanting with your eyes my walking trance.
Your love soon stopped, but one thing never ceased;
You always took me for your underpants.

When people stand about unclothed,
My shadow runs the other way.
'Commencing things' I've always loathed:
The pierce, the clash, the bloody fray...
The intervening times are best:
Between the strokes, swords poised in air —
To change direction, stop and rest:
Your rhythmic thrusts lie motionless there
Like fingers pressing down the keys
Waiting for the hushed vibrations
Those times my sister spoke with ease
Heart-felt love's communications.
So read between my lines, I pray;
My piano is a typewriter.
I press the keys and try to play

The way she played—but it was brighter.
And so I teach the little folks
That God was born in Bethlehem,
And other stories, games, and jokes.
They pay me, see, to lie to them
And paint the world all uncle-less
Without a single barb or thistle.
I make it simple, full of bliss:
"It's not hard work if you'll just whistle."
And, "No cow feels the butcher's knife;
Cows are made of leather."
"You'll have a free and happy life,
All happy together!"
And little can these kids suspect
That there's a sense beyond the six
Which only grown-up intellect
Can hang upon its crucifix
With things so sad they cannot cry
Or spare a tear for anyone.
Where wingless angels go to die
All shivering in the burning sun.
That we're just worms on our Creator's grave
Spending all our days in killing time
Which, deathless, cycles to the final wave
Smudging all our stiffened souls with grime.

Faces

As strangers must we meet, my friend,
in crowded rooms of three or more
where acts are played none comprehend
and conversation's just a bore.

But could we somehow meet alone
we'd pour ourselves in what we say
revealing how our hearts have flown
and hope to fly again someday.

We'd speak of sorrows, sympathize,
and tell our tales of ageless woes:
of love that comes and quickly dies,
of pain that comes and slowly goes.

But groups require a groupish face
that none may speak out frank and plain
but must disguise the harsh with grace
as one might cover up a stain.

We've different faces for each role:
a solemn face for holy days;
a sad, concerned one to console;
and one that looks entranced to praise.

I've got a face that has no ears:
just two big mouths and Cyclops eye.
I speak the blessing a friend hears,
but out the other curse and lie.

My groupish face is just a shield
I hide behind in apathy
with tender feelings all concealed;
expressions – painted, garishly.

But what a life when all's pretense!
My shield is rusty from misuse.
I want to put off all defense
give passion reign, let heart run loose,

and gather strangers called my friends
to see my daring exposé
when scissored truth with sharpened ends
rips my shield like papier-mâché,

and cuts a hole from chin to brow;
lets me be seen, and lets me see.
I'm stripping off my disguise now:
come view the thing that I call me..

New Glasses

You have new glasses, you tell me.
New frames... new lenses,,, helps you see...

I smile – your life seems so content.
Will you see new sights and visions?
Will our drab lives look different?
Shall we leave our home-made prisons?
Neighbor, will you live with flair
and journey on my madman's way?
We'll scale the mountains of Knowhere,
dance upon bright clouds of dream-day,
then float down the sky of sapphire
into the tranquil reason pools:
those lukewarm – half ice half fire –
middle-grounds which prove all men fools.
And every *Why* will be drowned out
as sound reasons touch our ears
removing each and every doubt.
We'll know why men must live in fear;
why greed is God and love departs;
why locks and bolts are required
on lonely neighbors' doors and hearts
shutting out all they desired.
Oh, the sparkling effervescence
of that longed-for joyous season
whirled by the passion of our sense,
flown on the wings of our reason!
But will our smiles still just reflect
hearts and minds yet waging war?
Such questions you don't expect;
After all, you're just a neighbor.
Neighbors, of course, don't see for *Why*.
Football scores, tomorrow's weather,
local gossip, a bright new tie...
these things are yours, and forever
you will be at home with these things.

You won't miss *Why*; you'll be content
with whatever ignorance brings.
I wish I could be ignorant
or wise enough to stand behind
your glasses or my smile.
I'd like to crawl inside your mind
and be you – or me – for awhile.

"They're nice," is all I say,
and we walk away.

Passing By

Passing on its way
I see it going by;
and when I see it
I always seem to sigh.

Life had passed me by
so early in my youth
that passing along with it
seemed always so uncouth.

And so I merely watched it
and soon I forgot
to pass along with it.
Did I miss a lot?

I watched it going by:
the passing parade.
For all its pageantry
but a dull charade.

Now I sit and I stare
at these old bones.
And the creaking floorboards
are my world of tones.

This house has been for me
a most dreary place
that never held a bride
nor a friendly face.

The rich dark woodwork
seems strangely now to bend.
Will you weep for me,
my melancholy friend?

Life will come in soon now:
in this room to spy
a man who has passed on
without ever passing by.

The Waiter

Contemplating a "Christmas" party - 1982

Why does he sit there on his hands,
the hors d'oeuvre tray naked,
while yet flows the spirit,
the night adolescent,
and the party loud?

It's because upon that tray
he carried his little self
in trembling hands
among the tooth-picked meat.

It's because no one took him;
preferring gut-stuffers.

It's because, at last,
only his little self was left
and they shooed away the tray
like a fly annoying them.

It's because
he opened up the perfume-caked window
to hear despair
and dropped his tiny soul,
craning to hear
over the gay laughter
the direction of his bloody feet.

Hopelessly Lost

At some point, very suddenly
the horrible realization comes.
The imperceptibly receding familiar
has now utterly disappeared
replaced with the *similar*
where everything shouts its wrongness.

Your reflection,
seen in warped blurs in the strange windows,
looks just like everyone else:
sullied and lifeless and routine.

But no matter how hard you scrub
the soul-deep dirt remains
mocking you and your little efforts
always
when you think you're in the clear,
you become aware of those shadowy figures
trailing behind you
constantly scrutinizing,
disapproving,
asking their eternal questions
and telling you with every turn
it's the wrong way.
And you shout back your blasphemy:

> *"Oh, to pull a Jesus:*
> *tip over their tables*
> *and whip them all out of town,*
> *strap on infernal wings*
> *ascend or descend –*
> *it's all the same*
> *as long as it's a flight*
> *away from me!"*

And all the angels, long dead,
laugh your defiance to scorn.
And God, bored to tears,
won't even waste a thunderbolt.
And so you continue to stumble,
walking in circles,
feverishly searching for the way out...
your life nothing but an embarrassment.

Last Dream

Sound: round dishes and bed pans together.
Sight: white, plucking eyelids like feathers.
Flowers drooping all about me color
the starch-white room shades of dying dolor.

And you, by the bedside, bring it all back:
your frown supplying memories I lack.
A certain near-death sensitivity
tells me clearly the tea sounds lukewarmly.
I smell bugs on the flowers as I say,
"Shall I tell you the dream I had today?"
With drawn-out sigh comes your reply
(which my ears somehow seem to amplify)
"Don't strain yourself, uncle, on my account."
(To which "Shut up!" seems to be tantamount.)
I smile, and shut my eyes, but still I see:
you glance guiltily at your watch, sip tea,
grimace, set it aside... and search for death.
Your eyes frisk my bed-sheets for signs of breath
and just when you think you've seen no breath flow
for several minutes, and stand to go,
I say, "It's no trouble at all, nephew."
And you slink back down into your "church pew"
thinking, "not over yet, this service odd,
not yet 'peace be with you, thanks be to God.'"

"I dreamed I loved a most radiant miss.
More than exceeding beauty, had she this:
a voice ethereal: music of the spheres!
(For her family had been that of Shakespeare's.)
Genevieve was her name, and as for me,
my family was of the great Houdini.
She acted out scenes like so many plays
while cruel tricks of fate filled all of my days.
In misty garden we did dwell
far from the city's man-made hell,

where, like Eden with Adam and his Eve,
I lived and courted fair Genevieve.
I crowned her the very queen of my heart,
and swore lover's oaths that we'd never part.
Rulers of the soil: 'garden royalty'.
Each day was an enchanted harmony.
We watched as green trees sugarized the air
and felt the breath of singing birds so rare.

Then one day a devil-bird swooped down
and flew off with my lady's golden crown.
So I climbed the tallest mountain for my love
with my eyes fixed on the demon perched above.
At the summit I clung with one desperate hand
and a foot away I saw the bird stand.
I grabbed the monster's claw to save my fall.
His strong wings lifted us into the blue,
it seemed the earth did fall away as we flew.
But I slipped and the ground came up so fast...
and lying with body bloody and gashed
I moaned to sweet Genevieve, "I'm not dead,"
which you heard and brought me to this sickbed.

Now he presses the button for the nurse;
he thinks I'm delirious and much worse.
Losing all: crown, life, love, and Genevieve,
it seems the time has come and I must leave.
Vulture death-bird! To wing away lives!
To tear apart love, and men from their wives!
(But was it real? Was Genevieve my wife?
But for this, dream or real, I might curse life.)

His breath comes short, his heart beats fast.
He's fearing this may be my end at last.
But I can hear now (a dying man's right)
what he would conceal with all of his might.
Secrets hidden from his very own mind
I need not seek – only listen – to find.

His wish, lying deeper than secrets lie,
cries out to me: "*Die! Die! Die!*"

To One Who Has Deemed Me an Enemy

We might've let each other in
had fear and pride not barred the gate.
The moment pricked me like a pin
when you declared defensive hate.

You struck at terror in my heart
as if it were a flint to light
some secret paper torn apart
and burnt to ashes in the night.

And since that time I've often guessed
what secrets made you act that way
to strike a fire in my breast
which put your faults on exposé.

For in the corners of your eyes
there dimly flickered fear and dread.
I saw in them were Satan lies
and demons dwell unlimited.

Perhaps if love had struck the flame
and lit up all your secret things
It would've changed the devil's name
and gave the demons cherub's wings.

The Businessman

Hyperbole fills all his days
like garbage in the landfill holes.
He speaks upon command, and stays
for promises of bigger roles.

Silent charts tracing inane trends
flash upon the colorless wall
in darkened rooms of backstabbed friends
with all for none and none for all.

His dreams are long forgotten;
he's sold his mind like a whore.
His insides are boiled rotten,
and every day there's something more:

like the boss he always humors
while he's gnawing on his bones,
or praying for malignant tumors
through his cellular phones.

Or else some fool may bring to mind
what all their mundane lives have cost:
deserted nature left behind,
and peace, and love, and paradise: lost.

The Janitor

My name is spelled *Anonymous*.
It's after time when I arrive.
My work is styled unglamorous
since nothing's pretty after five.

With toilet for a crystal ball
I could read their inner bowels,
or directly learn their all
tracing prints from paper-towels.

But such methods I deplore
when all about me, loud and fast,
down the walls the details pour
and haunt the night to daily past.

I know each face and family
as well as weights of each newborn.
The living are revealed to me
By pictures, checks, and letters torn.

I read the memos, bottles, trash…
the perfume lingers with the sweat.
I sniff my way through dust and ash
and trace the day in silhouette.

A day of action lies in state:
each can's a coffin for the chaff
I empty, winnow, and collate,
then simply read the epitaph

Shy Attack

He thought the purplish crawlers
were slimping out his ears,
and gawkish looks of passers-by
confirming all his fears.

His scagziness was bursting forth
into the realms around,
he heard his shivtilled stomach
make the gawfullest sound
till all the slurp-smiled faces
were peculiarly frowned.

His twandly arms would stick
in everybody's way,
and other parts would jut right out,
and that is how they'd stay.
He couldn't sleep at all that night
since it was still the day.

He thought his horns were blossoming
where everyone could see,
his clothes were his mirage,
or maybe stained with pcc.
He thought he stank and jellimeld
more than you or me.

He didn't want to North or South,
he couldn't East or West,
so hid himself as worst he could
amongst them as the rest,
and even had they spoke to him
he wouldn't have confessed.

* epilog *

The spoke of California,
a palace in the sun,
and never had they noticed him
from since he had begun.
But so he lived his snurkled life
until it all was done.

The Fisherman Views Creation

I will not sing of deep blue skies
nor of love for the sea;
for as the bird of heaven dies
the fish are killed by me.
And on the land all the trees *hurt:*
Through roots, imprisoned limbs
inanely flounder in the dirt
like a fish, struggling, swims
in vain to free itself from pain.
(To be unfettered – free –
is but a dream all dream in vain.)
Trees swimming hastily
are still caught by earth's hook of gore.
But I'm not innocent;
I caught a swordfish-sycamore
for sport, not nourishment.
I axed its trunk from off its head
and threw it and its scream
– which had me so disquieted
I sought for peace in dream.
But in my dream, with mighty swish,
a thousand trees fell down.
And in my dream a thousand fish
a thousand fish were drowned.
Scales of bark shone in slimy sap
on gore encrusted shore
which thirsty waters came to lap
then went away once more.

I still can hear the chilling screams
rise with the morning sun.
They echo my imprisoned dreams.
Oh, God, what have I done?

The Drunkard Views Creation

The sun sings its circular song
till twilight softly comes along
to start, with gently humming moon,
the sound of night – that haunting tune.
The somber moon-lit melody
awakes a cricket symphony.

Listen – thunder! (Angels' coughing.)
Tonight a storm's in the offing.
Trees sway, that's to say stagger,
as lightning drives its dagger
into earth's soft, yielding flesh.
The waters seep, and roots refresh
as thirsty things again are blessed
by liquid's ageless conquest.

The beauty of the night-time storm
makes me glad I'm safe and warm
inside this bar, atop this stool –
the object of all ridicule
for others think all creation
spells misery. Well, they may shun
it if they wish, but I forebear;
I see such beauty everywhere:
in each thistle, and in each weed;
in wounded animals that bleed;
in flies on fresh warm feces;
in tapeworm, fungus, disease;
in hemlock's taste, in scent of skunk…
but then again, I'm very drunk.

Street Scene

Like surrogated fantasies,
the sex-shop owner in his den
views triple-eXcess nudities
as means to some forbidden end
as, licking lips, stoops and devours
the slick and glossy photograph,
a slogan's heard: "No choice but ours!"
which mothers chant on our behalf
as they, on high, with picket beat,
decry the non-maternal breast,
Rambo slays across the street
with no one marching to protest.

A ten-speed whizzes past the scene
with biker's lungs of car exhaust.
A hoped for girlie magazine,
from shyness toward the marchers: lost.
The housewives share a common sigh:
too much pain with their pleasure lingers
to let the onan-artists tie
the world around their sticky fingers.
And lonely, would-be customers,
whom these same women scorned in school,
turn quickly to the theaters,
escaping scathing ridicule.
Since angels stand to guard from men
their only glimpse of paradise,
they learn not love, but war again,
attending Rambo's sacrifice.

Then, on to the abortion clinics
where mothers' homemade bombs are tossed
by former hippies now turned cynics:
the sexual revolution lost.
As Reagan, smiling down on them,
plants his own bombs in the sky;
in the name of peace he shall condemn
all non-reaganites to die.

Still Life

(The television-viewer as an object of art)

A clumsy artist's brush, too fast for art
is reaching out and scrubbing viewers' eyes.
But where does painting end, and viewer start?
Can anyone say where the difference lies?

If thought or movement be indicators,
the lighted tube must take the highest places
with grave-robbers and temple desecrators
for shining torch-like on remains of faces.

What would I see if I could turn around
and through this camera see them fettered there
with chains of thought, or like mummies bound
in dust that falls and winds from off their hair...

I'd see the cause of every vacant stare:
their eyes are blind from sponsors' labels,
their heads, long dead, retain a ripening air
like bowls of fruit on so many tables.

Numbers

Statisticians say
a great number die each day
from disease and accidents.
But I am not convinced.

I think it's a lie;
numbers don't die.
No, not at all;
numbers are immortal.

You can divide or subtract
or add what they lacked,
but they never end;
to infinity they bend.

I know it's not true;
it's me and you
and not numbers at all
that stumble and fall.

It's husband and wife
that depart from this life.
It's son and daughter
who die in the slaughter.

Words

On hearing of the death of a friend

Although I pay to hear it said
that life is full and hope is bright,
there's too much here that's gone or dead,
and I'm no God to set it right.

There are words I would say, by need.
Their burdens gladly I might bear
if only they would plant the seed
to wake me from this world's nightmare.

This heavy life's akin to sleep,
except that pain is always nigh,
and notlove flays and claws me deep
while gentle people have to die.

There are words I would say,
but I have challenged death before
and journeyed far on his broad way.
Yes, I have knocked on my tomb's door,
but no admittance did he yield.
So, should you love me right out loud:
I see this vast and withering field
of faces in a nameless crowd,
and horror cuts my eyes apart
to see them vanish in my place!
My tortured mind can't hear your heart
above each wasted, lonely face.

There are words I would say, by choice.
But they are words so bold and strong,
I'd need at least another voice
to sing them with me long and long.
I can't have such a one to love;
people die,
and, given all I've said above,
why don't *I*?

Janet

We who are left
by you
weep no more.
Beyond grief
(the long journey)
we wandered
aimless
as if the playwright of our lives
had abandoned the work
of making sense
and left us
to fend for ourselves
without the next act
or a principal player.

With the curtain still up
we stand here blinking
in the floodlights of a reality
which eluded you
and confused you with its meanness
and spun you around
with its old, familiar, dirty tricks.

They say to write you off
and get on with our lives.
They did not know you.
They don't understand
what lengths we'd go to
just to see your smile
once more.

We wish we could've rescued you.
We wish we would've known:
minds so trapped in other's prisons
often come to such decisions.

Richard Bradley

The Bradley's lived downstairs
in a house that wasn't theirs.
Sometimes I heard their fights
waged in the darkest nights.
Sometimes I heard their love
from my bedroom up above.

When I saw him in the daylight
Richard spoke of what was right.
He knew the Bible inside out;
a holy man without a doubt.

Richard Bradley was my friend.
To him my heart I did lend.
He spoke of life without woe
and made me want it so.

He sang a haunting refrain
that etched deep inside my brain.
He painted an illusion grand
from that Bible in his hand.

But the dream has long since shattered.
And the two of us — we have scattered.
Richard still dreams his dreams;
they're real to him, it seems.

Richard, Richard, where are you?
When I lost the dream I lost you too.
Where is the life we gave a start?
Where is my borrowed heart?

Weather-Beaten and Truth-Seasoned

Written by Cynthia Rose for Ted Evanston (both character in my book, "Falling in Truth")

I.
Out of a winter's death we rise
To new life in spring.
In sudden surprise
Truth-bells ring!
The thrill in our souls,
The ecstasy, the height,
Of reaching new goals
In warmth of new light!

II.
In the blazing summer heat
The light grows brighter still.
We put away milk for meat
And seek to do His will.
This heart of mine
In summer's youth
Feels the sun shine
And loves the truth.

III.
But should autumn ever come
And the light grow dim;
Should we lose the sun,
And should we lose Him:
Our hearts would sink
And cease to soar.
We'd stand on the brink
And seek no more.

IV.
When frozen truth-bells
Crack, and cease to Chime,
Our heavens turn to hells,
And truth's a dozen for a dime…
Then autumn falls to winter's death.
The pearly gates are frozen shut.
Our prayers are stuck in frozen breath,
Answered only by His "*So what?*"

What to Say to the Next Messiah on Your Doorstep or TV

Such a thing as *you* must *feign*.
What misery in these martyrs' roles!
Such minds must shiver with the pain
of glaciers sawing skinny souls.

I for one have tried to fight
the sparks that leap from off your pyre,
which scorches those who "see the light"
and burns them all in borrowed fire.

And you're so careful not to *"WHY?"*
or lose your blissful look, or scream,
that you can't hear the children cry
or taste another's golden dream.

The world that needs you you've forgot,
and since you quite refuse to wake:
the cross may bear you; I cannot.
I hope you die soon for our sake.

Moses

And Moses said unto them, "Have ye saved all the women alive? Behold, these caused the children of Israel... to commit trespass against the LORD... Now, therefore, kill every male among the little ones, and kill every woman that hath known man by lying with him. But all the women children, that have not known a man by lying with him, keep alive for yourselves."
Numbers 31:15-18

Now the man Moses was very meek, above all the men which were upon the face of the earth.
Number 12:3

Blessed are the meek: for they shall inherit the earth.
Matthew 5:5

Fished out of the depths
of the midnight of our subconscious,
plaguing disowned would-be parents
in fantastic rebellions
while always afraid
to even speak to them
except through a brother or god
by your side:

Meekest of men,
how you grasped
with thousands of hands
a promised inheritance
never gained.

Breaking
   stone laws,
   hymens,
   and necks,
you trod the people down
with tireless torches and swords,
heroically.

The first to tie devotion
in a blood-soaked package.
The first to turn racism
into godly genocide.

How could you know,
in your righteous zeal
for doing God's work,
someday Hitler would emulate you
against your own people?

The Murderer's Confession

When someone did me grievous wrong
I sought the Bible as a guide
for I've been told my whole life long
life's answers can be found inside.

I hoped to learn of toleration
in our dealings with each other
I'd search for just the right quotation
on how to make each man my brother.

So I read the Word of the Lord:
Moses gave His stern command:
"Put the children to the sword!
Rape the virgins! Steal the land!"

Certainly He had His cause
for killing every Canaanite;
someone broke immutable laws,
and punishment must make it right.

Such acts of murder, theft, and rape
aren't sins when God commands their doing:
Go get them all! Let none escape!
Carry out the Great Subduing.!

Thrilling as it was to read
of sinners getting recompensed,
it didn't really meet my need
and so I turned some pages hence.

Again I read God's Holy Word:
"Kill everyone within the city!
Let your sword be undeterred!
Upon the infants show no pity!"

Now surely He, who made us all,
commits no wrong in taking life
for God decides who'll rise or fall
who will kill, and who shall rape whose wife.

Enthralled, I turned and read some more:
"Rain pestilence upon the earth!
Immerse yourselves in blood and gore
and make your foes all curse their birth!

"Let none survive my godly wrath!
Pelt the Animals with stones!
Leave nothing in the aftermath
but smoldering ash and rotting bones!"

When children called God's prophets names
They might as well have mocked at Him.
God had such ones sent up in flames
or had them torn from limb to limb.

From Bible reading now I learn
to follow God's Eternal Plan:
How anger, greed, and lust can earn
sainthood for a wicked man.

When land or flesh were much desired
or someone's pride must be defended,
prophets could be quickly hired
to say this was what God intended.

Their consciences were swiftly soothed
by word or sign or sacred vision
which signified that God approved
their thieving, murderous decision.

And seeing nothing wrong in this,
the next time that I met my foe,
nothing, I thought, could be amiss
in dealing him a fatal blow.

For Us (With Love)

For the members of the ex-Jehovah's Witnesses Support Board.

We are dancing with our children
upon a grassy knoll,
or laughing loudly, hand in hand,
happily out of control.

We're Christians, pagans, atheists,
together in the sun.
We share a common history:
a freedom we have won.

We broke the chains that shackled us
within the blood-soaked halls:
burst out of mind-locked prisons
and climbed those tower walls.

Now we share a common journey,
saints and sinners all the same.
We don't agree on everything,
but that is not our aim.

We are here to love each other,
to share a laugh or sigh:
Arms for hugging, hearts in tune,
shoulders on which to cry.

We did not leave the truth,
we did not flee from love.
We simply learned such precious things
aren't ruled by those "above".

As for their threats of Armageddon:
we'll do more than just survive;
we'll not waste our lives in cringing fear;
we shall live our lives *alive*!

They swing their swords and hurl their hailstones
and hate us as they must...
Our love melts hail to gentle rain
and turns their swords to dust.

And when we're weak or lonely,
confused or in despair,
we have a place to come to:
there's someone here who'll care.

For you who languish still in prison,
in your endless passion play,
we have illumination;
we're here to light the way.

We offer understanding
to patch up all the holes
burned so deeply in your minds
and in your weary souls.

So join us in our zest for life
as we laugh here in the sun.
The joy is in the journey,
and we've only just begun.

Prayer of the Good Consumer

They tell us somewhere children struggle
  just to stay alive.
But with their letters, every day,
  new catalogs arrive:
with VCR's and stereos,
  CD's and televisions
(when weighed against our charity,
  these make for quick decisions).

Please help us laugh at those who wear
  compassion on their sleeve;
who tell such horrid tales of woe
  that no one can believe;
who march, and chant their mindless slogans
  only to protest
those necessary evils
  which bring us all the best.

Convince us the environment
  can handle anything,
that animals are only worth
  the pleasure that they bring,
that those concerned with suffering
  are evil terrorists,
and caring for the Earth's a plot
  contrived by Communists.

Give us this day a new cologne
  and omnipresent ad,
and tell us each annoying "cause"
  is just a passing fad.
We'll kneel before the cable box,
  and worship from our cars
till all the world's a pleasant blur
  of indistinguishable scars.

Deliver us from any knowledge
  of sweatshops and the like,
and punish those ungrateful men
  who unionize and strike.
We promise that we'll drink the blood
  of those who die unwillingly:
a strange communion with the dead
  who host our life's technology.

Reward us who have always known
  just where our duty lies:
who loyally consume,
  ignoring all fanatics' cries.
Assure us that our lives are blest
  by all Your Grace imparts
(despite the constant mouse-like gnawing
  deep inside our hearts).

Evergreen

Preserving thoughts of spring.
Keeping hope alive.
Enduring everything
just to survive.

Recalling the seed
against impossible odds:
the unyielding dirt, the choking weed,
the bones of dead fertility gods.

The single root grasping for existence,
the just-born shoot's fearless thrust
overcoming all resistance;
not knowing man, or greed, or lust.

But knowing mysteries no man knows:
how to live without having to kill,
and passively withstand one's foes
by being flexible, calm, and still.

Growing strong on hardship:
the needles sucking frozen sap,
the roots all cracked in ice's grip:
some Great Green God caught in a trap.

And untouched seasons somehow pass
and haul the years lie pall-bearers,
till, standing six feet over the grass,
it laughs at winter's terrors.

CHOP!
    CHOP!
        CHOP!

Never knowing the need to communicate till now
an electric scream shoots out the severed nerves.
The sap, like blood upon the snow: defeated somehow.
The tombstone-stump a glorious memory preserves.

Cadaver-merchants' merchandise.
Strung with price-tags and gaudy glass,
longing for the grip of ice,
hallucinating carpets into grass.

A thing so out of place – like God in hell.
But the fever fades – they wear out novelty
and consign it to the flames. "All is well;
it's a swell old custom," they say to me.

Will man, sitting in his luxurious chair of ease,
marking off the days, never hear the scream?
And standing on Bibles, computers, cars, TVs,
will he never reach the level of an evergreen?

The Rape of a Dream

On the occasion of the opening of the trans-Alaska oil pipeline

There are crimes of passion, crimes of lust,
there are times when judges are not just.
"Cut off the offending member,"
was never said (for I'd remember).
I've seen a sin pronounced a blessing
in the name of man's progressing.

I caught a thousand men engaged in rape
pounding their giant phallus into shape.
Like microbes of some strange infection
they worked non-stop. I watched the erection
across the virgin tundra's innocence.
I felt the monstrous strokes of violence
contracting with the freeze
expanding by degrees
burrowing through resisting soil
ejaculating the blackest oil
into the clearest streams and lakes
venom deadlier than any snake's.
The smothering film spread so thinly
it covered the snows of Mt. McKinley…

It's not just caribou and bears I see
coughing oil, blinking coated eyes; it's *me*!
It's my spirit that this thing pollutes,
for on this land I've put down roots.
She has nourished me and frozen me out,
she's raised immortal hope and mortal doubt…

And now the Valley of Ten Thousand Smokes
boils my blood and jealous anger provokes
to become the patron of her honor;
what right have they to lay this on her?
"Stand upright, Progress: meet your challenger!
For what great ends have you ruined her?"

As mighty ships begin their trek
with a million barrels on each deck,
I wonder what this child of rape will be:
some crippled, oily-skinned deformity
with pipe-line for a baby-bottle,
growing up with love for only 'throttle'
and 'acceleration', it needs a fix:
its bottle turns needle to give it 'kicks',
and when the oil flows in its blood
and its whole spirit's turned to mud
it will not see the ugly needle scars
it will not see or know a thing but 'cars'.
And when at last it's old and gone quite mad
with nature's gift of wise senility
it may recall a dream that once it had
which it proclaimed 'the land of the free'.

Yours to Use If You Choose

The billboards offer you kingdoms
to despoil at your whim.
Reduce you to a "consumer"
of certain demographic potential.
"It's yours," they say, "all yours"
to do with as you please:
wipe your feet on their faces,
tear the skin off their bleeding backs,
hunt them down or pen them up.
Slash and burn,
knock yourself out;
you're an American, by God!
Go snatch your birthright
with both fists
and a gun.
When you do as you choose
you can do no wrong;
all your actions are blessed
by Goddollar, in Whom we trust.

Flimsy Excuses

"It's the way I was raised."
(*Typical response to the question: "Why do you eat meat?"*)

They start out in the nursery
  with tales by mom and dad:
hunters rescue little girls
  by shooting wolves so Big and Bad,
while a duty-bound, remarkably efficient
  farmer's wife
mutilates disabled mice
  with her husband's carving knife.

You know they're not as real
  as Santa in his fur-trimmed coat
whipping harnessed slaves:
  the reindeer straining to stay afloat
(whose job it is to serve mankind
  and never shirk or tire
while dragging home the massive weight
  of all that we desire).

In Sunday School they preach at you:
  humility, abasement,
and of our LORD and Father
  (a Santa Claus replacement)
who loves, with flared almighty nostrils,
  the smell of burning flesh
(especially when the body's warm
  and still is kicking fresh).

Who, as a perfect man,
  to demonstrate his power
multiplied a school of fish
  for humans to devour.
Who showed who's boss
  by driving human demons into pigs
and showed what nature's for
  by cursing trees for lacking figs.

They hand you worms, and hooks with barbs,
  and grandpa's fishing pole:
you learn to lead the dance of death,
  enjoying the control.
You hang your victims out to die,
  and pose for photographs
as grownups slap you on the back
  and brag on your behalf.

You watch that clown on television:
  mirth he will arouse
while serving up your happy meal
  of butchered, smiling, cows,
and when you eat their murdered flesh,
  you certainly conclude
that animals were born to serve;
  they're merely walking food.

You try to imitate your dad,
  who knows and understands,
whose judgment you respect
  much more than any other man's.
Standing by the kitchen sink you'll have
  a son-and-father chat
as he drowns unwanted kittens
  minutes out of your old cat.

In school they pass out frogs and scalpels
  stored upon the shelf;
they say that it's the only way
  to learn about yourself.
When you relate your expertise,
  your dad makes a decision:
next Thanksgiving you're to make
  the ritual incision!
But as you dine upon the heart
  you've proudly just cut out,
I wonder if you'll ever come
  to entertain a doubt
about a life's philosophy
  which best is paraphrased:
"*I cannot change because it's just*
  the way that I was raised."

The Hunters

Silently at last they crouch
the beer rumbling in extended bellies
squinting one-eyed through crosshairs
hearts pounding, adrenaline pumping.
Memories of a night spent in tall tales
and laughter and fellow mockery.

The fawn, unaware,
nursing on the grazing doe,
hears an unfamiliar sound
as pain rips open the insides of her mother.
She flees in fright

alone

as strange creatures
with long detachable smoking phalluses
run to her mother and slice her open.
And hunger and fear compete in the little body
"saved from starvation"
by the strange predators.

Later, while the head of the doe's mate
adorns the office of the well-fed highly respected
boisterous businessman buffoon,
the snow gently falls
to cover a single shivering form

alone.

The light extinguished in those eyes
shall not be seen again.

Melrose Minnesota

"Home of Jennie-O Turkey Meats"

Elephants, the myths contend,
have picked the place where they all die.
But *men* have picked the spot to end
the lives of birds denied the sky.

A bloody funnel Melrose is,
through which the turkeys pour.
For all the lives it closes,
its gaping mouth wants more.

Here, mothers thrust their baby's heads
beneath the dripping, mashed remains,
to suck the lifeblood from the dead,
and learn dependence on the slain.

The automated butcher's tool
engulfs the streets with blood.
Bespattered children wade to school
through a growing man-made flood.

Mechanically, each teacher starts
espousing economic needs,
till brain-sliced pupils all impart
a blessing on the butchers' deeds.

The people here have learned their place.
They do not look through turkeys' eyes;
they know they're of the Master Race
for whom all other species die.

The farmers are hard-hearted wardens
of torture-cages overcrowded
with guiltless prisoners no one pardons
in a system few have ever doubted.

The truckers take birds to the road
beneath a sky they've never seen.
They stack them up like any load
and haul them to the death-machine.

The workers hang them on the lines
suspended by their feet.
The shoot a voltage down their spines
then watch them hacked up into "meat".

It's all for no one but ourselves:
exhuming frozen turkey graves:
the supermarket's bloody shelves
which stock the flesh that we all crave.

But no one is responsible,
and no one is to blame.
No one feels uncomfortable,
or hangs their head in shame.

Song of the Last Animal

With eager hunters drawing near
I hugged her more protectively.
She gazed at me with eyes of fear
and whispered her last song to me:

"I'm the last of all the animals
who'll ever live on earth.
The last to feed the cannibals
who ruled our death and birth.

It was rain and sun, thaw and freeze,
it was branches, leaves, and dung,
the sparkling lakes, the buoyant breeze,
which filled the ancient songs we sung.

All those songs, with us, are done,
and only smog and metal wings
will rise up to the sun,
and fly across your silent springs.

For it's been countless bloody seasons
since the humans all arrived
who had their morals and their reasons
which none of us survived.

Who made up for their every lack
by slash-and-burn and massacre,
and ripped the skin right off our backs
because they had no hide or fur.

Who crammed their face-paint in our eyes
because they were ugly and odd,
or took our life in sacrifice
because they'd sinned against their god.

Who pierced our flesh with lead and hook,
and sentenced innocents to prison,
or stood dumbfounded as they'd look
and never see our sacred vision:

a vision of life without their walls,
of homes, unpaved, uncaged,
of freely running without stalls,
of dying naturally, and aged,

in a world without the dread
of those who called themselves humane
as they'd shoot us in the head
or dine upon our last remains."

To His Former Psychologist

No longer do the dreams come
true
all our birds lie
dead.

The streets run straight
now
and speak of fast death
more quietly.

Most people have mouths
a few have eyes
there are no ears
yet.

I have checks, a phone, a car:
the trappings of a person
infected with
normalcy.

I did all those things
you suggested
and even believed in your
happiness.

I lunched with a woman
once
pretending I was you
horribly.

I work hard
daily
and try to fit
in.

My phone's unplugged
as I write this
so I can think of you and
remember

How we made contact
nearly
and how I shrank away
back inside

Saying, "I am well,"
agreeing
lip-service to my ashamed
family.

No one knows
to this day
that I'm insane -
(least of all you)

And death is all my dream
and I curse
my dreams no longer
coming true.

To His Future Psychologist

What would it be like
if, when I meet her,
it is *she*:
the savior of the world,
decked in flowers and supplications,
twining out all my illusions
into one straight, strong
umbilical cord
through which she passes me
her love and wisdom?
On such nectar
might not *any* man live?

Joe "the grinner"
(megalomaniac in Painsville insane asylum)

I've got New York inside of me
and I refuse to set it free.
Odor of trash and sewage-slime
rise from my bowels like foul crime.
Keep It Clean signs stuck in the mud
float from view on my own black blood.
A drunken man sleeps in the park
while muggers lurk there in the dark.
A kind of fear and guilt pervades
like knives between my shoulder blades.
All the politicians' lying
cause city-rot. Putrefying
from all their corrupt wicked ways,
the flesh around my mouth decays.
My spleen's a ghetto, heart's a slum,
and Harlem's in my cranium.
The rapists, thieves, and whores combine
to knit the cord inside my spine.
The sounds of nightlife: disco, jazz –
all of them interrupted as
I hear the screech of subway trains.
Cockroaches swim through bloated veins:
hair-legs scratch arterial walls
as blood-pressure rises and falls.
Eggs hatch en masse – we co-exist.
I sometimes watch them in my wrist
scampering over each other,
while in my lungs they make me smother.
One fell out my nose yesterday
and it started to run away.

I caught it and put it back in:
that's why I'm here, and that's why I grin:
I've got New York inside of me
and I refuse to set it free.

Martin Potter (paranoid schizophrenic in Painsville insane asylum)

---

she always looked out dark round windows
vaseline hands and naked clothespins
amazing grace and the cratered moons of Jupiter
slipped between her fingers
concrete in her skull
long deep sigh longer than that
like the mushrooms on the ceiling
they're not allowed in 5th storey apartments
she kept the cow hidden in the umbrella
tired feet and meters gas man came
raining manure
but the only stools were toad
gas put me to sleep
i woke up to a party in the tomatoes
i should've known from the way she held parsley
i saw god there above the bowl
with blonde hair on her crude knife
the mayonnaise fell from out of the sky
the guests forming worlds of green
were tossed and eaten for their sins
god disappears sometimes
but i hear his wings fluttering in the wall
keeping pain alive and martin lutheran
inkpot melted bright green
now look at the floor
i stood atop the devil's head
as he rose he smelled sweet
his horns were thorns
his tail a root
and the garden earthly delights
i went to get some
i held one in my claw
my claw! my claw! my claw!

honey poured from my moustache
bible hates honey
your face in its mirror
with honey on your lips
shame guilt sin
i broke the mirror without superstition
our god hates that book
worlds exploded translucent spheres
broken face rabbits eating their eggs
virgin mary had abortion
flies healed on jesus butt
jagged dark window
brains oat mealed in the street.

Suicide Note #1

A mystic wind took hold of me
and blew my mind afar.
It carried me till I could see
the back of every star.

Ahead of me was nothingness;
behind me, not much more.
I wondered which contained more bliss
and which I should strive for.

When through the blackish murky deep
I felt a kind of peace:
oblivious contented sleep
in which all cares did cease.

Comparing it to all my days
of worry and of woe
I think I'd rather sleep always
than back to life to go.

Suicide Note #2

Love is not some soft sweet thing
such as songs are written of.
Brilliant birds, unpitying
swoop unseen, and such is love.

Sharp — the pangs of hearts grown cold.
Hard — the world outside my dreams.
Gone — the love I used to hold.
Far — the god my soul blasphemes.

Suicide Note #3

If I go to sleep and die
in the morning I won't cry.

But I dread to wake from sleep
for I know I'll weep and weep.

Life's a song, or so they say,
but I'm filled with such dismay:

Can I really wake and sing
having failed at everything?

I've been waiting much too long
for this note to end my song.

Suicide Note #5

The time has come
and I'm alone.
It's all right;
Time says it's all right
as I crawl back inside
its historic arms.
And time's a gift you gave to me:
there was a moment when I saw you:
the first tick.

Before that,
they asked me to:
  dance without legs,
  laugh without a smile,
  think without a mind,
  live without love.

Back then I dreamed of you.
Back then the sky was always black,
the birds did not fly,
I was alone and cold
without the strength to cry.

Out of wishes you appeared
and gently took my hand,
breathing words of sweet love.
Your sighs pricked the sky
and all the stars showered down.
All things grew wings
and sailed beneath the whispering sun.

We dreamed together.
Sometimes our astral selves
paraded across the cosmos
while streams of light-bodies:
fire-souls,
sparked essential truths,
and down our blue selves
marshmallow dreams escaped:
mini-fogs around our feet:
train-steam
to mingle with the rails of infinity.

And now you're gone
and I'm alone.
It's all right;
the Night says it's all right.
And the night seldom cracks anymore
spilling its ancient intestines
upon my bed;
I had a doctor fix it.
Now it only groans slightly
as I fall into Time's embrace
deep inside of it
until

the six A.M. dog barks
and I didn't die again.
I recall your eyes
and curse your gift
shaking a fist at the daytime's
iron sky with

car-farts

and
dead birds

frozen in mid-air.

The day is here
and I'm alone.
It's all right;
the Day says it's all right.
Its belly sings forevermore
of painful truths:
ax-and-sandpaper reality:

"It was notlove."

I plead with tears and words,
and all-night talks, and inside-jokes,
with midnight dancing,
with bedside manners,
and thick and thin,
and thought and touch...

"It was notlove."

Day yawns a gaping mouth,

"For all of that, it was notlove."

Suicide Note #6

I've sat here long, and through these hours
my mind, in vain, has tried to clutch
the loss of love, of stars, of flowers.
For, all old dreams were made of such.

And where's it gone to? Where's it flown?
And why is notlove so severe?
And why are hearts now made of stone?
And what am I still doing here?

The Classical Composer's Disillusionment

A universal vision — yet my own:
in fields of green a palace grand,
where Music, Queen of Muses, had her throne —
where she reached out and took my hand!

Sweet goddess, loved by all, to think I kissed
the lips Tchaikovsky kissed, and felt
the arms that held your lovers Brahms and Liszt
in the lands where Beethoven dwelt.

The butterflies flit, the flowers grew notes,
the birds sang tonal fugues divine.
My love and I transcribed their trilling throats
a note each day; each month a line.

Till twenty years of perfect music were writ.
Then Music brought an urn of brass,
she smiled an put our flowered notes in it.
— And then the strange things came to pass:

A beetle crawled onto her neck and dug
into her skin with awful sound
(Then it sprouted eagle's wings — no more a bug)
the blood that trickled down her gown
made sounds peculiar to immortal blood,
attractive through their novelty.
And from the trees a million ears did bud
demanding more of cruelty.

All nature's savageness came into play:
rocks rolled — a jagged stone nicked her —
all discipline and practice went away
— the only scales now were Richter.

The whole world heaved and out came Satan's bands!
What a horribly splendid sight!
Possessing the animals and the lands:
Three dogs did her in one cold night.

The million ears all loved her dying moans
mistaking them for melody.
And now they're deaf to any other tones
except the wind whistling through her bones
and tendons trembling mournfully.
There's none to wail her death but me.

The butterflies have petrified to iron.
The flowers crushed by Zeppelin's lead.
The world I had is ashes in my urn,
the result of devo.,
which, if Music did know,
she'd be so grateful to be dead.

King Futility's Decree Against Poetry

Hooray! Hooray! For poetry is dead!
The proclamation: "Away with all verse!"
Shall be read in the towns and heralded
throughout the world: throughout the universe!

And this is what my message shall contain
— For I, myself, am author of the plan —
Away with all flowery speech: speak plain,
Like roses speak to honey-bees of fields utopian.

Away with big words you have to look up!
Away with anthropomorphism,
About which even dogs and cats are fed up!
Away with all proverbialism!

He who write poetry
Shall never see a thing;
He hides reality
In his absurd rhyming.

It is hereby declared a crime
To write a couplet in a rhyme.

Away with all alliteration and assonance
That take tongues twisting and turning towards
Some stupid sentence such as assaults an ass's sense.
(Like lewd lusty looks at ladies insults the Lord's.)

Away with metaphor and simile.
Let these old smelly fish fade away
Like Pisces drowns in daylight's sky of sea,
Let wordless sun shine on unmetered day.

The Answer

If man were perfectible,
if you could just take one
that was correctable
and strip him to his skeleton,
rewire his brain so some synapse
brought logic to both hemispheres,
enlarge the frontal lobes, perhaps
the cerebellum too (thought clears!),
and then if you could speed his heart
to idle more efficiently,
economized his air transport,
gave all his flowings resiliency,
and made reflexes lightning quick,
gave feelings and all that they imply
(for this, indeed's, the hardest trick:
to let him pity, love, and cry)...
If then you'd speed his learning so
his IQ. score would jump the scale:
with joy of life he'd overflow,
seeing through each moment's veil.
You'd clothe your man in beauty-skin:
a supple roundness to the frame,
with room for life to grow therein,
and strike the spark of love to flame
till it would kindle tenderness:
every virtue it would fashion
until "potential limitless"
through a heartfelt compassion.
He'd be all mankind's brilliant hope,
and, given station, he would shine:
the light for we who blindly grope!
World peace and plenty he'd combine!
You'd surely make his life span grow
if you could start before the bones
and just before the embryo,
and give him *two* good chromosomes.

Then, in the nine month interim,
as it were,
if you ask me what to call him,
call him "*her*"!

The Weary Scholar

Have you seen the learned men
whose minds go round and round again
and wind up where they started from
without a law or rule of thumb?
You may have seen them in a dream
for learned men are only seen
by fools whose sight is so much clearer
that they can see them in a mirror.
I sat upon the "ivory tower";
my seat was sore within the hour.
"Is what exists what I am seeing?"
And "What is truth?" and "Where is being?"
With questions such as these I've striven;
for each one asked no answer's given.
But here's a saying with truth in it:
"There's a *seeker* born every minute."

My temples bore the weight of *Why*
(a pain no aspirin can belie.)

But wait, I'll be more laudatory,
for learning's mankind's crowing glory:

I think a mind's a splendid thing,
but crowns should never wear the king.

Whatever Happened to Streakers?

Whatever happened to streakers
who ran with nothing but sneakers?
They once were all the rage —
made many a front page.
But now I never see 'em.
Are they stuffed in some museum?
So I made up my bitter mind
to call on that editor blind:
Did what he print reflect *his* taste,
or was *any* news therein placed?
He looked at me with shifty eyes
and asked me, "Just who qualifies
as a streaker, my dear sir?"
I: "I will first hear *your* answer."
He: All the news that's fit to print."
I: "All the nudes that's fit to sprint."

Index of Titles and First Lines